LIZZO and ARETHA FRANKLIN

Queens of Soul

Tim Cooke

Lerner Publications ◆ Minneapolis

Lerner Publications Company
An imprint of Lerner Publishing Group, Inc.
241 First Avenue North
Minneapolis, MN 55401 USA

For reading levels and more information, look up this title at www.lernerbooks.com.

Main body text set in Eurostile LT Pro.
Typeface provided by Linotype.

Library of Congress Cataloging-in-Publication Data

Names: Cooke, Tim, 1961- author.
Title: Lizzo and Aretha Franklin : Queens of soul / Tim Cooke.
Description: Minneapolis : Lerner Publications, 2024. | Series: Musicians and their inspirations | Includes bibliographical references and index. | Audience: Ages 8-12 | Audience: Grades 4-6 | Summary: "Aretha Franklin and Lizzo are inspirations to their generations. But Franklin was an inspiration to Lizzo first. From reinventing musical genres to empowering women and people of color, young readers learn more about their lives"— Provided by publisher.
Identifiers: LCCN 2023046314 (print) | LCCN 2023046315 (ebook) | ISBN 9798765626702 (library binding) | ISBN 9798765629116 (paperback) | ISBN 9798765635766 (epub)
Subjects: LCSH: Lizzo, 1988-—Juvenile literature. | Franklin, Aretha--Juvenile literature. | African American women singers—Biography—Juvenile literature. | Singers—United States—Biography—Juvenile literature. | Rap musicians—United States—Biography—Juvenile literature.
Classification: LCC ML3930.L579 C66 2024 (print) | LCC ML3930.L579 (ebook) | DDC 782.42164092/2 [B]—dc23/eng/20231004

LC record available at https://lccn.loc.gov/2023046314
LC ebook record available at https://lccn.loc.gov/2023046315

Manufactured in the United States of America

1 - CG - 7/15/24

TABLE OF CONTENTS

Introduction

In 2018, Lizzo was in the studio of Atlantic Records. She was recording her third studio album, *Cuz I Love You*. On the studio walls were photographs of Atlantic's greatest stars. One was singer Aretha Franklin. In the 1960s and 1970s, Franklin was known as the "Queen of Soul."

Lizzo's real name is Melissa Viviane Jefferson. She started going by Lizzo when she was fourteen.

Franklin found fame when she joined Atlantic Records in 1966.

Franklin's photographs inspired Lizzo that day. The singer decided right there that she wanted to be the Aretha Franklin of her generation. She wanted her new album to be great. She wanted people to listen to her music years for years after it was released. Lizzo dreamed that this would be her breakthrough album the same way Franklin's iconic album *I Never Loved a Man the Way I Love You* was for her.

CHAPTER 1

Hitting it Big

Franklin's and Lizzo's musical careers began in church. Both went on to become big stars.

Growing up, Franklin sometimes toured churches around the country. Her dad was a minister. He was a famous singer. Franklin's mom was also a singer and a pianist. Franklin grew up in a musical family. She followed her dad on his national tours and sang in his choir.

When Franklin was eighteen, she switched from singing gospel music to singing pop music. She moved to New York City, New York, to work with Columbia Records. For the next ten years she tried all kinds of music, from blues to pop. She struggled to achieve success with audiences until she moved to Atlantic Records.

Franklin's love of gospel music continued throughout her career.

At Atlantic, Franklin went back to singing gospel-blues music. She recorded her tenth studio album, *I Never Loved a Man the Way I Love You*. It was an immediate hit. The album sold a million copies. It was the breakout the Queen of Soul had been looking for.

Franklin's career lasted more than fifty years. She went on to sing more genres, from disco to dance tracks. As the decades changed, she followed the trends in music. "Music changes, and I'm gonna change right along with it," she said.

I Never Loved a Man the Way I Love You *was Franklin's first album to reach the top ten on* Billboard*'s top 200 albums.*

INSPIRING THE INSPIRATION

The Ward Singers

Lead singer of the Ward Singers, Clara Ward, helped inspire Franklin's career. In the 1950s, the Ward Singers were the biggest female gospel band in the US. The Ward Singers often toured with Franklin's father. Franklin got to see up close how Clara Ward made sure the band looked glamorous. The Ward Singers often wore sequined evening gowns and wigs. It was a look Franklin later frequently copied.

In 2022 Lizzo played a 200-year-old crystal flute that belonged to US president James Madison.

A Skilled Musician

Lizzo's family were members of the Pentacostal Church. Growing up, she often sang gospel music at home and in church. In fifth grade, Lizzo started to study the flute. She played in her high school's marching band. At the same time, she rapped, wrote songs, and started bands with her friends.

After graduating high school, Lizzo went on to study music at the University of Houston. Her flute skills earned her a scholarship. But by her third year at the university, she decided not to complete the course. "I was like, 'I'm already performing. What do I need a music performance degree for?'" she said. "And I just stopped."

Lizzo's big break came with her third studio album, *Cuz I Love You*, released with Atlantic Records. Since then, she has performed at the 2023 Glastonbury Festival. She also sang the title song for the 2023 *Barbie* movie.

Lizzo performs at the Glastonbury Festival in 2023. She and her dancers wore matching green wigs for the main act.

COOL CONNECTIONS

Both Franklin and Lizzo struggled to make it big with their original record companies. They found more success after they signed with Atlantic Records.

CHAPTER 2

Songwriters

Franklin and Lizzo have different approaches to songwriting. Franklin often sang others' songs or co-wrote them. Lizzo writes all her own songs.

One of Franklin's biggest hits was the song "Respect." It was a cover version of a song by singer Otis Redding. Franklin did many cover songs, or songs that were originally performed by others but that she performed with a new spin. She sang popular covers of songs such as "Bridge over Troubled Water" and "Crazy He Calls Me."

In 1968, Franklin and her then-husband wrote the song "Think." The song was one of the few that she helped write herself. It was about women who had been mistreated by their partners. Franklin wanted the song to help empower women. "We all require and want respect, man or woman, Black or white," she said. "It's our basic human right."

Franklin was best known for singing songs written by other musicians.

Empowering Songs

Unlike Franklin, Lizzo writes and produces all the songs she performs. For her breakthrough album, *Cuz I Love You*, Lizzo wrote almost 170 songs. In the end, she chose just twelve of them to appear on the album.

But like Franklin, Lizzo's music aims to empower people, especially women and people of color. In some songs, she approaches them like she's writing an essay with examples and arguments. In others, she writes about her life and thoughts on body-shaming, sexism, and racism. Her music is a mixture of rap, ballads, and dance music.

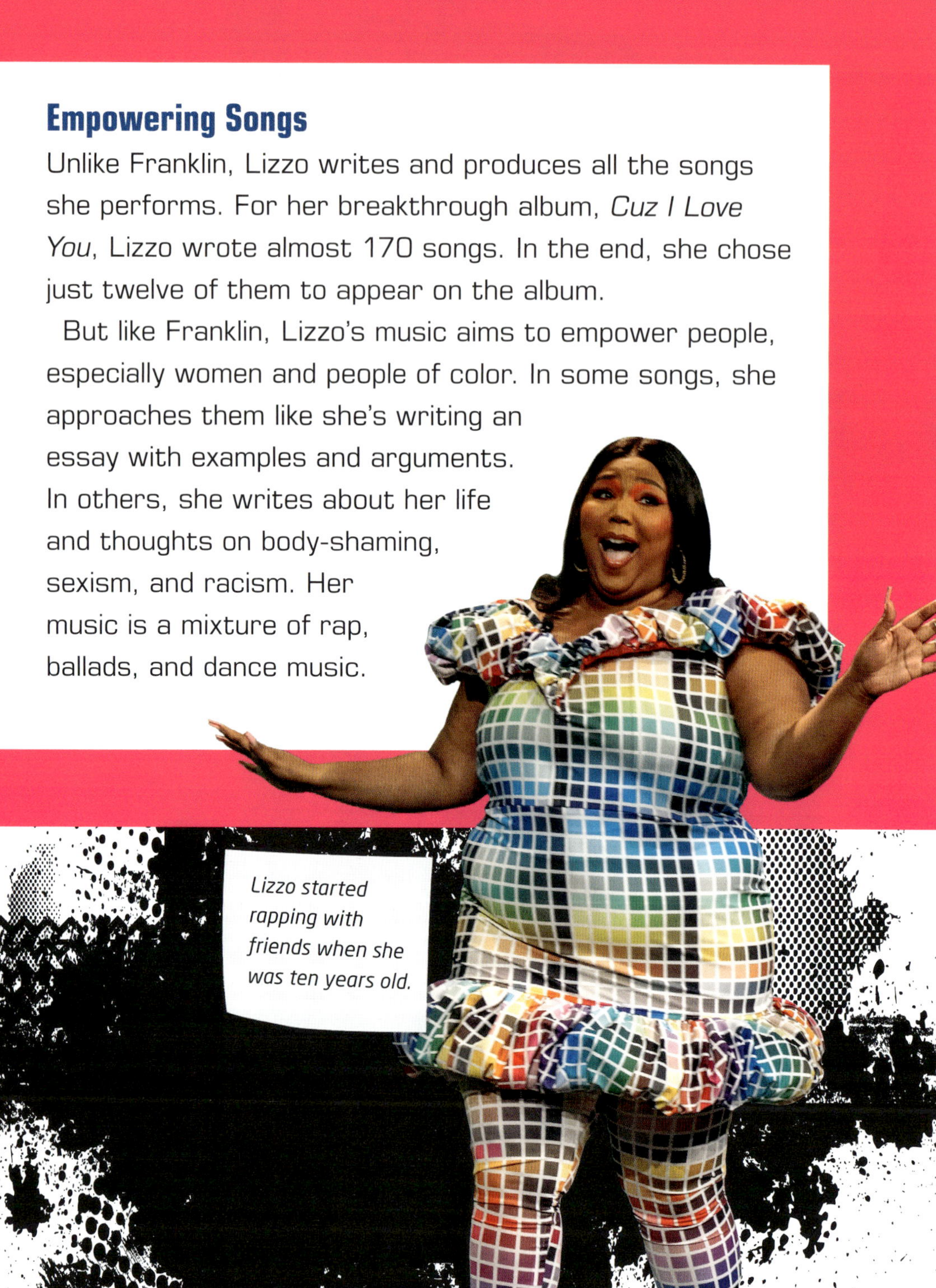

Lizzo started rapping with friends when she was ten years old.

COOL CONNECTIONS

Lizzo made the album *Cuz I Love You* as a tribute to Franklin. While she was recording it, she asked herself what a rap album in 2019 by Franklin might be like.

Before *Cuz I Love You*, Lizzo found it hard to use her full vocal talent in her songs. She felt that many Black singers were thought of as "belters," people whose voices were powerful and strong but not very musical. She didn't want to be put into a box. By this album, she felt more comfortable with her voice.

Lizzo often writes about her relationship with her own body.

CHAPTER 3

Shine on Stage!

Franklin and Lizzo are very different live performers, but they both share one rule. The more sparkle the better.

When she was young, Franklin learned from the Ward Singers the importance of a strong stage presence. Part of this included dressing up. Franklin wore long and short dresses with sparkling jewels, sequins, and fringes. Her outfits were highly visible. This way, even fans at the back of the concert hall could see her.

Sometimes Franklin played the grand piano as she sang. But most of the time, she simply stood up and sang. Her backup singers and band performed behind her. She did not need many props. Her voice alone made her shine.

Franklin sings on the TV show Solid Gold *in 1983.*

Franklin often wore elegant evening dresses similar to those the Ward Singers had worn.

Franklin sang for President Obama at his 2009 inauguration (left) and in the White House in 2015 (below).

Over Franklin's career, she performed with many musicians, from Ray Charles to Mariah Carey. She also sang at many important occasions. She sang at Martin Luther King Jr.'s funeral. Presidents Jimmy Carter, Bill Clinton, and Barack Obama all asked her to sing at their inaugurations.

Dress to Impress

Lizzo adores wearing clothes on stage that sparkle. "Fashion is an extension . . . of my creativity," she says. Lizzo wears anything from tight leotards to fitted dresses. She's a proud advocate for body positivity. For the Special Tour, she wore specially made full-body catsuits, covered with sparkling stones.

Lizzo's stage clothes range from fishnets to colorful wraps.

Lizzo and her dancers perform high-energy dance numbers during concerts.

High Energy!

Lizzo never stops moving during her concerts. Her shows are full of nonstop energy. On stage, Lizzo is surrounded by dancers, backup singers, and musicians. She and her dancers move to the music and pump up the crowd. Sometimes, she plays her flute too.

Most of Lizzo's crew are women. They wear bright clothes to go with what LIzzo wears. Lizzo loves to involve the audience. She gets them to sing along.

COOL CONNECTIONS

President Obama is a fan of both Franklin and Lizzo. He attended a 2015 event where Franklin sang "(You Make Me Feel Like) A Natural Woman." In 2019, he named Lizzo's "Juice" as one of his favorite songs.

CHAPTER 4

Earning Respect

Franklin and Lizzo have both had successful careers. They've won awards and received musical honors—but they also gave back to their communities.

Franklin's career lasted almost sixty years. In 1987, she was the first woman to be inducted into the Rock and Roll Hall of Fame. She won eighteen Grammy Awards across her career, including a Grammy Living Legend honor and a Lifetime Achievement Award. Franklin had 112 singles in the charts and sold more than 75 million records.

In 2005, the Queen of Soul received the Presidential Medal of Freedom. The award recognized her contributions to music and her work in the Black community. Franklin supported many causes. She gave money to the Civil Rights Movement. She also donated to food pantries and raised money to support inner-city kids in Detroit, Michigan, her hometown.

Franklin received many awards, including the Presidential Medal of Freedom in 2005 (above).

Franklin's honors included having a street named after her in Detroit.

Using Fame

In 2019, *Time* magazine named Lizzo its Entertainer of the Year. In 2020, Lizzo was nominated for eight Grammys and won three. However, the singer uses her fame to do more than just promote her music. She also uses it to draw awareness to issues she's passionate about.

Lizzo attends the 2005 MTV Awards.

In 2020, Lizzo attended the Brit Awards in a dress based on a chocolate bar.

Body Positivity

Lizzo encourages people of all body types to do the things they love. As a person with a larger body type, she shares her thoughts on body-shaming. Body-shaming is when people make inappropriate or negative comments about a person's body size or shape. Lizzo encourages her fans to be body-positive instead.

COOL CONNECTIONS

Both Franklin and Lizzo have made appearances in movies. Franklin appeared in the film *The Blues Brothers*. She sang her hit "Respect." Lizzo stars in the documentary film *Love, Lizzo* (2022).

Being Inclusive

In 2022, Lizzo started a reality TV show, *Lizzo's Watch Out for the Big Grrrls*. It set out to find the best big dancers for her upcoming tour. Just like her inspiration, Aretha Franklin, Lizzo wants to create an inclusive community.

Lizzo meets her fans at the 2017 Treefort Music Festival in Idaho.

Your Inspiration

Franklin always wanted to sing. She knew she had been given a special gift. Over the decades, she used her success to help people less fortunate than herself. Causes such as the Civil Rights Movement and women's rights were very close to her heart.

Lizzo has been inspired not just by Franklin's voice but also by her readiness to take action. Lizzo uses her fame to support women and people of different body types. She wants people to respect each other and be inclusive.

Who inspires you? They don't have to be someone famous. It could be anyone: your best friend, your teacher, your aunt, or a person in your community. Why do they inspire you? What can you learn from them?

IMPORTANT DATES

1966	Aretha Franklin signs with Atlantic Records.
1967	Franklin releases her album *I Never Loved a Man the Way I Love You.*
1987	Franklin is the first woman inducted into the Rock and Roll Hall of Fame.
2005	Franklin is awarded the Presidential Medal of Freedom.
2015	Franklin sings at the Kennedy Center Honors concert in front of President Obama.
2018	Lizzo records her breakthrough album, *Cuz I Love You*.
2019	*Time* magazine names Lizzo Entertainer of the Year.
2022	Lizzo launches her own reality TV show. Lizzo starts her tour for her fourth studio album.
2023	Lizzo performs at the Glastonbury Festival in England for the second time.

GLOSSARY

advocate: a person who supports a cause or group
blues: a type of music first sung by African Americans, generally expressing great sadness
body-positive: having or showing acceptance and appreciation of all body types, including one's own
body-shame: to judge someone negatively because of the shape, size, or appearance of their body
Civil Rights Movement: a movement for racial equality in the US that arose during the 1950s and 1960s
cover: a version of a song originally performed by someone else
empower: to give someone strength or power they did not have before
genres: styles of music or other kind of art
gospel: a style of Christian music
studio album: a collection of songs recorded in a place with musical production equipment
tribute: something done as a mark of respect to someone

SOURCE NOTES

8 Norman Jopling, "Aretha Franklin Stops to Think: A Classic Interview from the Vaults," *Guardian*, March 20, 2012, https://www.theguardian.com/music/2012/mar/20/aretha-franklin-classic-interview.

10 Colin McEvoy, "Lizzo," Biography.com, Updated August 3, 2023, https://www.biography.com/musicians/lizzo.

12 Pubali Dasgupta, "The Pioneering Figure of Aretha Franklin," *Far Out*, Accessed October 27, 2023, https://faroutmagazine.co.uk/aretha-franklin-the-pioneer/.

19 Aiyana Ishmael, "Lizzo on 'The Special Tour' Outfits, Creativity, and Wardrobe Malfunctions," *Teen Vogue*, December 15, 2022, https://www.teenvogue.com/story/lizzo-special-tour-interview.

LEARN MORE

Britannica Kids: Aretha Franklin
https://kids.britannica.com/kids/article/Aretha-Franklin/632647

Britannica Kids: Lizzo
https://kids.britannica.com/students/article/Lizzo/636519

Felix, Rebecca. *Lizzo: Singing Superstar*. Minneapolis: Big Buddy Books, 2022.

Kiddle: Aretha Franklin Facts for Kids
https://kids.kiddle.co/Aretha_Franklin

Lizzo: Official Website
https://www.lizzomusic.com/

Markovics, Joyce. *Aretha Franklin*. Ann Arbor: Cherry Lake Publishing, 2023.

Murray, Tamika M. *Aretha Franklin*. Lake Elmo, MN: Focus Readers, 2023.

Wilson, Lakita. *Lizzo: Breakout Artist*. Minneapolis: Lerner Publications, 2021.

INDEX

PHOTO ACKNOWLEDGMENTS

Image credits: David Lee/Wikimedia Commons, p. 4; Atlantic Records/Billboard Magazine/Wikimedia Commons, p. 5; Atlantic Records/Wikimedia Commons, p. 7a; alisafarov/Shutterstock.com, pp. 7b, 23c; Blueee77/Shutterstock.com, p. 7c; Stefano Chiacchiarini '74/Shutterstock.com, p. 8; Skyhawk/Shutterstock.com, p. 9a; Gyvafoto/Shutterstock.com, p. 9b; Everett/Shutterstock, pp. 9c, 23a; Library of Congress Life/Wikimedia Commons, p. 10; Raph_PH/Wikimedia Commons, pp. 11, 20a, 20b; Mark Reinstein/Shutterstock.com, p. 13a; Hadrian/Shutterstock.com, p. 13b; Daniel Benavides/Wikimedia Commons, p. 14; Adam McCullough/Shutterstock.com, p. 15; Michael Bush/Dreamstime.com, p. 17b MediaPunch/Shutterstock, p. 17a; Cecilio Ricardo, U.S. Air Force/defenseimagery.mil/Wikimedia Commons, p. 18a; The White House/Wikimedia Commons, p. 18b; Taylor Creek Media/Dreamstime.com, p. 19; Ron Foster Sharif/Shutterstock.com, p. 21; Paul Morse/georgewbush-whitehouse.archives.gov/Wikimedia Commons, p. 23b; Featureflash Photo Agency/Shutterstock.com, p. 24; Featureflash/Dreamstime.com; p. 25a Fred Duval/Shutterstock.com, p. 25b; Treefort Music Fest/Wikimedia Commons, p. 26. Cover: Raph_PH/Glasto2023/Wikimedia Commons; Michael Bush/Dreamstime.com.